Plums, Stones, Kisses & Hooks

A Breakthrough Book
No. 35

Plums, Stones, Kisses & Hooks

Poems by Ronald Wallace

University of Missouri Press

Columbia & London, 1981

University of Missouri Press, Columbia, Missouri 65211
Library of Congress Catalog Card Number 80–15907
Printed and bound in the United States of America
All rights reserved
Copyright © 1981 by Ronald Wallace

Library of Congress Cataloging in Publication Data

Wallace, Ronald.
    Plums, stones, kisses & hooks.

    (A Breakthrough book; no. 35)
    I. Title.
PS3573.A4314P56   811'.54   80–15907
ISBN 0–8262–0314–0

for my family

Acknowledgments

Grateful acknowledgment is made to the editors of the following publications, where many of these poems originally appeared:

California Quarterly, "Bullhead" and "Hippopotamus"; *Carolina Quarterly*, "Drowned Children"; *The Chariton Review*, "A Concise History of the Twentieth Century," "Down on the Farm," "Dying," and "In the Cave"; *The Chowder Review*, "The Medicine Man's Confession"; *Epoch*, "Tossa: Celebration"; *The Iowa Review*, "Bat" and "One Hook"; *Kansas Quarterly*, "Making Do"; *Midwest Quarterly*, "The Real Thing"; *The New York Quarterly*, "Bottom's Dream"; *The New Yorker*, "Oranges," copyright © 1976 by The New Yorker Magazine, Inc.; *The North American Review*, "Breaking Away," copyright © 1975 by the University of Northern Iowa; *Northeast*, "Cleaning House"; *Northwest Review*, "Prayer for Fish"; *The Paris Review*, "Extracting the Honey"; *Perspective*, "Lost in Woods"; *Poetry*, "Installing the Bees," "In the Apiary," and "Pastoral"; *Poetry Northwest*, "Building a Workbench," "Into the Cascade Forks," "Love Song for My Father," "Recognitions: Grindelwald," and "Triumphs of a Three-Year-Old"; *Poetry NOW*, "Trapping the Last Fox"; *Prairie Schooner*, "Grief," "Tomatoes," "Trout," and "Zucchini," copyright © 1975, 1976, 1977 by the University of Nebraska Press; *Quarry West*, "In the Tetons"; *Quarterly West*, "Feline" and "Spring Again"; *Sou'Wester*, "Intensive Care" and "After Being Paralyzed from the Neck Down for Twenty Years, Mr. Wallace Gets a Chin-Operated Motorized Wheelchair"; *The Wisconsin Review*, "Microcephalic," "Microcephalic (II)," and "Cucumbers."

"Installing the Bees" was reprinted in the Borestone Mountain Poetry Awards Volume, *Best Poems of 1976*.

"One Hook" was reprinted in *The Ardis Anthology of New American Poetry*.

Some of these poems appeared in a chapbook, *Installing the Bees*, published by Chowder Chapbooks.

I wish to thank the Wisconsin Arts Board for a fellowship, and the Graduate School Research Committee of the University of Wisconsin–Madison for a grant that helped me while I was writing these poems.

R.W.
Madison, Wisconsin
12 September 1980

Contents

IV. Trout

V. The Moon and Our Own Devices

I. Installing the Bees

Installing the Bees

First this: a thousand bees
balled up in one black heart,
a loud wind, a fist of heat,
locked in their thin cage,
edgy with energy.

You carry them out to the hive,
gently, their delicate balance
locked in your dangerous hands,
gorged with your sweet words,
the sky buzzing with dusk.

Then this: the hive like a white thumb
stump on the frozen land.
You open it slowly
and pour the bees out,
as if an escarpment, a sluice.

Now the bees seethe and roil.
You slap down the cover, suddenly
frightened at the weight
that falls from your arms,
the splash of dark waters.

You lift your white hands
to your eyes, waxen, honeyed,
pale lilies, mums, the dead man's
flowers, a thousand bees buzzing
in your wrists.

In the Apiary

Sleepy with bees,
the sun leans back
on the stand of oaks.
Blossoms buzz in the orchard.
The beekeeper, protected,
his swart face veiled,
his hands full of smoke,
opens his noisy hive.
A few bees line up
on the edge of the frames
wary, suspicious,
twitching their bad intentions.
When the first bee stings,
goes on about its death,
the beekeeper flicks it
off with his hive tool.
He is immune by now, he thinks.
It will not affect him.
When the second bee
gets under his veil,
lost in his blind eye,
and the third goes straight
for his heart, the beekeeper
calmly replaces the supers
and walks back to the house,
his long gloves heavy with summer.
Later, after supper,
as he watches his stings
go down with the sun,
as he watches the night start to swarm,
he remembers his several deaths.

Dying

1. Williamsburg, Iowa

I drift back in center field
and camp out
under the last fly ball,
smacking my lazy mitt.
We're ahead; the whole team
leans toward the dugout;
the visitors start
to pack up their bats,
the catcher unclasps his protection,
when suddenly my eyes
curve in toward my head,
my legs forget their intentions,
and the sky goes dizzy with stars.
The whole team draws its breath
until I am flat on my back
in the spastic grass
looking up at a web of raw faces.

2. Iowa City, Iowa

Each doctor is certain
the others are wrong.
My friends agree: alcoholism.
They walk me out
from under my legs.
They hand me their pity
and a cane.
My clients, suspicious, grow thin.
My son and daughter shudder.

3. Ann Arbor, Michigan

Multiple Sclerosis. The word stumbles
in my stumbling mouth,
or follows me at a safe
distance. Until, one day
it kicks out my cane,
sends me sprawling in wrong directions.
It slides me into an awkward chair.
My hands grow wheels, turning.

4. St. Louis, Missouri

I'm lecturing on jurisprudence.
The catheter jams, and a slow stain
spreads on my pants.
A girl in the back row snickers.

* * *

Alone in this dark house.
I listen to ballgames
race through my ears,
replayed on their good legs.
The T.V. turns itself on
and off. My wife, my children,
my eyes will not focus.
The needles and tubes attend me:
sclerosis, they say,
the suicide squeeze,
the glove on the spine torn off.
Called on account of darkness.

14

Love Song for my Father

I watched my father's legs break up,
the brittle shells suspended
in a sea of wheelchairs.
Oh, I hated him. And then

I felt my father's voice uncurl,
his words like suckers
wrap around my ears,
his needs grow thick
and weedy. I could not swim
out of them. And then

I watched the minnows of his eyes
finally turn white belly up,
his thought turn limp
and aimless as a jellyfish until
he could not raise his hands
above a whisper. And then

I could not follow him
no matter how I tried.

After Being Paralyzed from the Neck Down for Twenty Years, Mr. Wallace Gets a Chin-Operated Motorized Wheelchair

For the first time in twenty years
he is mobile, roaring through corridors,
bouncing off walls, out of control,
breaking doorways, tables, chairs,
and regulations. The hallways stretch out
behind him, startled, amazed,
their plaster and wallpaper gaping,
while somewhere far off,
arms spastically flailing,
the small nurses continue to call:
Mr. Wallace . . . Mr. Wallace . . .

Eventually he'll listen to reason
and go quietly back to his room,
docile, repentant, and sheepish, promising
not to disappoint them again.
The day shift will sigh and go home.
But, in the evening, between feeding and bedtime,
when they've finally left him alone,
he'll roar over to the corner
and crash through the window
stopping only to watch
the last geese rising,
rising by the light of the snow.

16

Intensive Care

Like breathing under water,
his short breaths treading
the liquid in his chest.
Too weak to cough,
he can barely stay afloat.
I turn on the suction,
pull on my rubber gloves.
Now I slip the tubing
through his nose
and down into his throat.
His face gags and stumbles,
his eyes wide for the first time
all day, held open by
the cold thumb of terror.
Why? he pleads, the word
in the air between us
like a barrier. I push
the tubing through it
into his chest. *Cough!*
I shout. *Jesus, cough!*
But he cannot.
The tube slips into his stomach,
into the digestive juices.
When I pull it out,
it stings his raw nose
like an eel. I try again.
This time I get into a lung
and suction it, the thick
persistent mucous and blood,
pneumonia's cold proof.
He wants to cry, *leave me alone.*
For Christ's sake let me die.
I try not to listen.

Now, he breathes easier.
I wipe the still blood
from his nostril
and lower him back in the bed.
Now, slowly, he floats
away from me into sleep,
beyond my good intentions,
growing smaller,
now father,
now dark shape,
now shadow on the water.

Grief

for my father

Finally, there is no hope.
Bandaged with grief,
that sweet, reliable poultice,
I leave you, exhausted, confused,
reaching out into the half-light,
mechanically gathering up air.

Outside, it is night.
I imagine the earth itself is heavy
as if the sky, too, were weeping,
as if the pale moon were some kind of proof.

But pure grief eludes me
for all its exquisite simplicity,
until I see myself carrying
not your death in my arms, but poetry,
this poem, this sad bastard child,
this terrible arrogance of art.

Now I place my hands on my face, trembling.
Now I weep.

In the Cave

When I have been here seven days
I lose my eyes.
I spend hours reading the dark
with my hands,
looking for clues.

At fourteen days
my ears shut their lids.
Inside my head
I find only the dark
sound of my heart dropping
like water on rock.

At three weeks I forget
where the center is.
My tongue, thick as a bat,
sends its signals out.
Nothing comes back to me.
Nothing bounces back.

A month and I am lost beyond
my eye, my ear, my tongue.
I settle in, remembering
stalagmites and stalactites,
all those moist-eyed lovers
growing slowly toward their deaths,
groping toward each other
in the dark.

A Concise History of the Twentieth Century

1900

Suddenly you see
a buzz saw, screeching
like an owl,
circling down, down
upon the small mouse
of your thumb.

1910

Your grandmother dies.
You bury her in
the basement.
One night you hear something
breathing, bursting
from that old root.

1920

You grow rich.
Money works for you.
Then, you smell
something burning. You begin
to sew like crazy.
You grow poor.

1930

You dream about it
all day. Finally
it's time to go home
to your wife and the dog
waiting for you,
their long tongues hanging out.

1940

You go out to gather the eggs.
Something is disturbing
the chickens; their cackles

strike you like cross-fire.
You hit the dirt.
Shells burst all around you.

1950

You're kneeling at the
communion rail.
The pastor white and
pungent as bread, his thin
lips full of blood. You
will not swallow it whole.

1960

Your daughter grows up.
Her nipples sweet as buds.
That night you dream
of bees. You remember
you are allergic as
they settle on your sleep.

1970

Your son pulls out
his gun. You can see
he's had it hidden for years.
He begins to shoot.
You can't tell if he's
dying or smiling.

1980

You grow cancerous.
People leave you
to yourself.
Soon, there is nothing
at all startling.
You wouldn't be surprised.

II. Oranges

Oranges

This morning I eat an orange.
It is sour and juicy. My mouth
will tingle all day.
Ouside, it is cold. The trees
do not anticipate their leaves.
When I breathe into my hand I smell
oranges.

I walk across the lake.
Ice fishermen twitch their poles until
perch flicker the surface, quick
and bright as orange slices.
The sun ripens in the sky.
The wind turns thin and citrus,
the day precise, fragile.

My mustache and eyelashes freeze.
When I arrive at your house
you are friendly as a fruitseller.
We peel off our clothes, slice through
that wordy rind.
When I lift my fingers to your lips:
oranges.

Tomatoes

Are in the air,
ripe and peppery.
Here. Eat one.
We have plenty.

The vines with their
green hair
sing to the fall air
tomatoes, tomatoes.

The wind is full of salads.
It runs into your ears
and down your chin.
Listen. You are a child again,

drooling your first teeth,
pulling up your roots,
wrapping your demands
around great stakes.

And now, your voice
takes hold and ripens,
peppers the clear fall air:
tomatoes.

Zucchini

There is a shortage of bees.
The zucchini blossoms refuse
to pollinate.
The vines grow huge,
cumbersome, and bare.
I ask old Mr. Lockhart
down the road.
He never says much,
just shakes his head
with palsy or impatience,
and goes on about his chores.
I wish I were back
in the city, in a store
full of zucchini.
I walk home alone.
The next day, Mr. Lockhart
is out in our garden
with the blossoms, copulating,
sticking one inside another
in a parody of love.
I shake my head, ignore him,
go on about my chores.
Weeks later, though, I find
zucchini everywhere: in the corn,
under cabbage leaves,
in a bundle at my door.

Cucumbers

In the far stall the old sow,
heavy with farrow, snuffles in her sleep,
her rough teats stiff as funnels.
We shovel manure, make room for a new litter.
Heavy and wet, the odor roots through our noses,
its thick snout poking down our throats.

Days later, the manure will be dried out,
rotten. We will spread it on the cucumbers,
to fatten up that sweet fruit.
And in August, after harvest, crisp and ripe,
the cucumbers will slice up, squealing under the knife.
We will suckle on their rindy juice.

Extracting the Honey

Wrapped up in canvas, rubber, and gauze,
we walk out to the hive.
It is August, and hot.
The sun stings us through our thick gloves.
When we lift up the cover:
a brisk wind of bees.

We pry through the propolis
and loosen the supers.
All summer we have not talked.
We brush clean the sagging frames.

Back at the house
we slice the wax caps off
and crank up the extractor.
The honey flows, limpid and gold.

Our hands slick and sticky,
we strain out the bees' legs, feelers and fuzz.
We open our difficult mouths.
Now our tongues turn to honey.
For the first time all year we are
giddy with our sweet lives.

Mother and Child, Rocking

She holds you to her breast; you are
a wrinkled sack of promises,
a small rag of flesh, sucking.
It is dark. Outside, the trees
reach out for the night,
holding their own,
while the orioles and goldfinches,
those bright children of daylight,
flicker. Spring: the forsythia
stiffened in its buds,
the pussy willows frozen
to their stems, the staghorn sumac
brittle on its stalk,
all begin to rock. Until
the moon fills with milk,
the thin stars glistening as if
the sky itself were liquid,
pressing us up to them
this thirsty evening
at the long end of winter:
rocking, sucking, together now, rocking,
forsythia, goldfinches, sumac, full moon,
mothers and children, rocking.

Triumphs of a Three-Year-Old

Winking

Her whole face wrinkles up like an apple doll,
a dishrag, a small clenched fist,
her lips thin and twisted until
the eyelids of one blue eye kiss. And then
her face breaks bright as water,
her new smile smooth as milk.

Whistling

She stares into the mirror, her lips
stitched in knots, dumb as a fish,
dry bubbles rising from her lungs.
She wishes harder,
her small breaths hissing like a teapot.
When one thin whistle finally slithers out,
she carries it downstairs carefully,
holds it up for us to see.

Nose-blowing

The kleenex covers her face like a large white bird.
She tries to brush it away,
but it flies back, dry, persistent.
She knows her father is behind all this,
so she starts to cry, her swollen eyes
fluttering around the room.
There is nowhere else to go;
the white bird's toes crawl up her nose:
she blows.

Shoe-tying

The shoelaces hang limp as worms.
When she pokes them with her fingers
they quickly squirm away from her,

burrow into her dark shoes.
She digs them out, determined now,
her fingers clumsy as hooks.
Later, I find her, smiling,
rowing around the house, her shoes
strung from her fists like fish.

Tongue-clucking

The mysteries of the mouth,
that wet place shelled with teeth,
the tongue, blind as a yolk,
sticking its blunt nose out.
She sucks it in; it begins to cluck.
We feed it words of encouragement.
It grows. Begins to crow.

The Ballet Lesson

White tights and tutus,
sequins and gauze,
can I say swans?
Not gliding, not flying,
no swimming, no song,
but bouncing and tumbling,
clumsy, now running,
now jumping, now
leaping in air,
hands flapping, undismayed
by gracelessness, weight,
now smiling, now shouting,
confusion and noise,
until
the teacher glides in,
quiet, poised,
her breath high and feathery,
her small hands perched limp
at her wrists.
The music begins,
and she's dancing, pale
mother, pale swan,
her small ducklings
jumping, now fluttering,
now rising in air
like, god help us, music,
like swans,
and *I'm* flying,
in back with the fat grandmothers,
dour fathers and wives,
I'm shining and smiling
right out of myself,

beyond reason,
back to childhood,
to light, until
I notice them staring.
I come down.
I return to my chair,
to my smile,
to my years.
Tendu. Tendu, close.

Down on the Farm

We live in the country so long
it becomes predictable.
The cows all hold their shapes;
the fields stretch out, indifferent;
the farms, farmers, tractors, sows,
conversing like characters
in an old book.

Then, one day, you drive out
from the city. We shout warnings.
We say: things are not as they seem!
You ignore us, drive down
the road's long tongue,
into the mouth of the huge cow
of sunset. It grows dark.

You want to cry out, but who
could hear you,
in the stomach of this old cow?
Fear stretches its long roots
inside you, aching to blossom,
the first bud of a scream
poking from your throat.

Meanwhile you hear us above you, plowing,
arranging the strange harvest.

Pastoral

In this stiff cornfield
the stunted ears
erupt with fungus;
the burdock wields
its seedy mace;
even the bees turn bitter,
guarding their honey.

We cut the hay,
riddled with thistles,
milkweed, sudan grass.
It sticks in our lungs.
The sun goes down faster
and longer.

Here on this hot day
we wonder why we came
to this abrupt country,
locked in its seasons,
a stiff wind telling
our fortunes
from the north.

III. Lost in Woods

Microcephalic

September: I had carried you all summer,
heavy in the heat, names
flitting through me like bright birds:
Joshua, Benjamin, Katherine, Emily.
Emily: you were a perfect baby,
red as a maple leaf, your face
full of finches and flickers,
your bald cry signing the air.
Yes, I heard the doctors say
from somewhere far away. Yes . . .
Outside, the winter
settled in, dry and bitter.

Meanwhile, you grew quickly.
Soon, you were smiling, waving
with your small fists, lifting
your head toward the future,
turning your new body over, sitting up,
thinking of your first steps.
Outside, spring thrust up its first fingers;
gray geese returned to the marsh,
the bloodroots and tulips reviving,
the crocuses waking up.
The whole world was growing, taking note.

Until April: the doctors said
microcephaly, craniosynostosis,
the words tightening their sutures inside me,
fluttering like strange arctic birds.
And then you began to grow backward,
beyond me, rolling over
through your short past, unraveling
that thin strand of months:
now sitting, now turning, now lifting

your head, now smiling, now crying,
a frightened, blind mouth, calling
for me to come find you.

June: outside the geese fly south;
the sun loses touch with the frost;
the bloodroots and tulips slip off
softly to sleep, the nights
growing longer for keeps.
And now you are pinned to sleep.
And now you are too small to see.
And now I stare at your absence, in silence.
My heart full of old names,
dry leaves, and gray birds, I
carry you thus through the summer.

Microcephalic (II)

The pressure is unbearable, as if
I were being born again and again,
my head perpetually stretched out of shape,
my small brain flattened against my skull.
They wonder why I cry so much.
Safe in their own large spaces,
they watch me, my face pinched and twisted
in a frown. I wish that I could tell them.

Some nights, inside sleep,
I grow toward all the places
they had imagined for me:
my tiny brain dropped from me like a frog,
my clumsy body turned delicate as a kiss,
the past, that crafty stepsister, left behind,
my mother and my father, found,
and grown so fond of me.

But then the sun glares in reproachfully,
the birds begin their clatter,
and I wake up, trapped in their painful faces,
back in the body of this shrunken dwarf,
counting the gold he has lost.
And then I cry, oh, I cry,
until they lift me in their hard,
unremarkable arms.

At the Horicon Marsh

Milkweed pods burst and rattle in the wind.
The sky is covered with fuzz.
My daughter, running through marsh grass, scatters
    seeds.
Overhead, the geese squawk, melancholic, plaintive,
as if a thousand children crying in the breeze.
Far off, shotguns, muffled and blunt.
My daughter asks what they mean.

As I explain, the afternoon turns cold and dark.
The red sun bleeds on the horizon.
The sky grows teeth.
And she is in my arms, holding tight,
her small voice burst wide open:
she will not stand in the rattling grass.
She will not run after the geese.

I hold her, but she is growing heavy.
I will have to let her down.

Drowned Children

If in March or November you see them
floating free through the thin scrim of ice,
far down at the bottom of winter,
aloof in the taciturn season,
blue and permanent, their lips slightly parted,
their white teeth perfect and new,
their hair gently furling the current,

remember: the cold water will slow down their
    breathing,
their small hearts beat but once in a year,
their blood huddle warmer within them,
passive and natural as fish.
You may yet blow your confusion back into them,
warm them to your urgent concerns,
bring color to their white, quiet lives,

but their sweet death may come back to haunt you
with its stiff persuasions
each autumn as you grow older,
holding fierce to the shore,
the child in you floating deeper,
the last summer crumbling
in your hands.

Lost in Woods

I look for moss
on the north side of your voice
while the little birds in your eyes
peck at me.

My fingers, like wood mites,
long to go exploring;
my tongue would carve initials
on your bark.

My thoughts grow dark.
And we are lost in woody dreams,
no moss, no sun, no green imaginings
to tell direction by.

Our fond intentions
gone to brambles:
your voice, my fingers
grasping, scratching.

Breaking Away

You know this dream.
You walk out of your house one night
wiping your family off of your mouth
like a bad dinner.
Moving through the dark streets
you feel your daughter's cries
slip out of your ears and fly away,
tame as a bedtime story.
Your wife grows smaller and smaller,
her belly filled with stones.
You are free at last
and alone.

Meanwhile, the street
lifts you on its tongue.
The night grows wings.
In the distance you hear
your wife and daughter singing,
their voices reaching out for you
with long fingers.
You feel yourself slipping
but it's a long way down,
your heart blown in,
your thin smile glowing
like a bone.

Into the Cascade Forks

First your Bic pen loses its ink.
Then at the next bend
your fishing pole disintegrates,
leaving you alone with your hands.
Words slip away elusive as trout.
Your car keys drop out through a hole in your pants
gnawed by your own thin fingers.

Slowly, columbine takes over the trail,
raising its own fragile notions.
A moose comes out from behind your eyes
to browse. You lose your clothes.
You are clean at last, and alone.

Then, clouds begin to accumulate
like bad ideas. A rock cocks its head.
The lodgepole pines lean toward you
scratching their chins, the rapids noisy as traffic.
Then, the whole valley trembles
on its green feet. The clouds lift up
the corners of the meadow and flip you into the air.
Higher, higher, the wind grown thin, and cold.

In the Tetons

Slithering out of the mountains,
swallowing trout, the Snake River
hisses and twists. Dawn.
A bull moose maneuvers
through fields of balsamroot,
prairie smoke, lupine, scarlet gilia,
and pauses at the river's edge, feeding,
obliterating the sun.
Stalled in this still dark,
small and incomprehensible, I shiver
for one long moment,
forget why I am here:
the Tetons quietly rising up behind me,
some thin trout twisting,
splitting the silver air,
a dark moose chewing on the sun.
And then, the day takes shape,
predictable, expected, the river
and the mountains settling down,
the moose a dark imagined shadow
vanishing in the sun,
my spinning reel singing
in the clear, accustomed air.

Spring Again

The aspens glisten
like new silver
dollars. The plum trees
spend their blossoms.
Spring, the costly season,
is back in town again,
passing its bad money.
And like a sucker
down on his luck
I ask to be taken in.

IV. Trout

Bullhead

I feed in the mud. My head
is one dark thought after another.
If you bait your hook correctly
I will probably bite.
I am always hungry
for love.

Come at night.
I will be waiting, available
as a bad idea.
When you think you've got me
firmly in hand
rip the skin off over my spine.
Then, slit the belly open
and abort the pouch of eggs,
that wordy gelatin.

Be careful when
you remove the head:
I can sting you with my horns
long after I am dead,
and the loud wound can fester
for weeks.

Bat

Wrapped in a leathery
sack of wings
the bat clings upside down
behind my eyes,
sleeping.

It is dark.
Far in the trees
beetles are conceiving
ideas. Crickets lift their legs
and saw thin syllables.
Words complete their tunneling.

The bat stirs
in my stirring hair,
stretches its wings
against the dark,
singing.

I shape myself
around its mouth.
Now, the claws reach out
and take hold,
drawing their blood
from my tongue.

Trapping the Last Fox

First make friends. Tell him
you can be trusted. Get to know
his bad habits. Then,
find a hill in northern Pennsylvania
and set your trap. Bait it
with your own worst intentions.
Do not move anything.
Even a weed will give you away
at the slightest provocation.
Now, open your bottle of fox scent
and sprinkle it around.
The breezes will assist you.
Move off into your own country
and wait.

        When you hear the fox
barking your name as if it had been
passed down for generations,
move quickly. Prick a small hole
in the base of the skull
and slip a bullet in. No one
will even notice. Then,
pull the skin off over the ears,
and stretch it from here
to your childhood.
Ignore the little fox pups
following you around like lies.
You have imagined them.
They are nothing like a fox.

Feline

Locked up, inside,
I have been watching
spring come on
for weeks now, when
one day my owner
opens the door
and I slip out,
quiet and flat as a shadow.

I am no more than
the slight breath of my passing,
a gust of wind in the grass.
I blend into the hedge
and watch the shrubbery flutter,
the branches crackle and spark.
And oh, I am graceful,
I am sly. Safe
in my leafy disguises,
I watch the day go by.

I am so attentive I can sense
the ants and beetles going on
about their hard business,
the joy of the spirea, dancing,
the dandelions spreading
their delicate messages,
the plum tree conjuring its blossoms.

Now confident and sleek,
I preen from tree to tree, mysterious,
pouring myself out of myself like water.
I am a butterfly, a grass blade, a plum
blossom, a bee; I leap, I shine, I
fly in the dangerous air.
I know I could live here
gentle and fierce forever.

And then, the crows unmask me,
the gray jays cry me naked,
and my owner arrives,
his hands full of promises and pain
and brings me down.
And now we are back in the house,
safe with the tamed oak and maple,
behind these predictable walls,
watching spring angle gracefully
away from us
on its soft impossible paws.

Recognitions: Grindelwald

You will know it's Frau Baumann
by the way the morning laundry
shakes her out to dry.
Or if she's in the garden
how the weeds pull up her fingers.
Every day the hay around the chalet
rakes her shoulders with slow strokes.
You will notice that
she carries winter on her back
like a hump your heart would weep for.
And every summer evening
you can see her thin limbs
prancing to the wind chimes of her cows
on higher pastures.

Tossa: Celebration

They are having a fishing contest. It is a holiday. All the local fishermen put down their mended nets and take up their poles. The women, dressed in black, bandanaed in sweat, watch.

It is a relief not to have to get into the small boats one day out of the year. It is a relief not to have to catch a boatload of fish. Just one. Shoulder to shoulder, they throw out their lines, reel in, their sure hands brown and wrinkled in the sun.

An old fisherman at the end of the beach has a big one on the line. All the children run over to watch as he plays it slowly in. Then, everyone laughs, returns to the other poles. It is a squid. Nothing good. The old man shrugs his shoulders, and holds up the squid, stretching its tentacles against the sun. Red, gray, and green it glistens. He laughs. It is beautiful. He slaps it against a rock, and drops it into his pail.

Cleaning House

September, old charwoman, arrives at your house
dragging the northwind behind her,
disturbing the bright sparks of cardinals,
sweeping the fall sky clean.
Out on the lake, the waves slap
their white hands together, keeping warm,
while the pike, stiff as knives,
slide deeper to sleep. September, Wisconsin.
You breathe in the ice storms and blizzards,
the clean skies below zero, the long nights
with your wife and the fireplace
remembering their warm intentions.
You feel this September enter your head
to sweep up the clutter of summer:
its tractors and grackles, its harvests and roots,
its skies stuffed with sunshine and pollen.
So this is September, efficient, precise,
buffing the bright trees to color.
She takes up your time, folds it neat
in the closet, and leaves you so clean
you almost forget you've grown colder.

Prayer for Flowers

Show me the disguises of coral root
that I may go unnoticed among enemies,
the tenacity of columbine
that I might thrive in the unlikely place.

Teach me to climb higher than envy,
to trust my own colorful seasons.
Let the wind move me; let me keep my roots.

Like the pitcher plant let me store up rain
against the dry season, surviving with patience
whatever comes along.
Show me the wind's song through lupine
that my blue days may be filled with music.

Teach me the persistent delicacy of glacier lilies
that I might endure winter's cold, heavy foot.
And, at the end time,
neither stiff-lipped nor trembling,
let me go up, like bear grass,
in a puff of smoke.

Prayer for Fish

Twenty below. It is too cold
to talk. Words break in the air.
The tips of my fingers crack and split.
My ice auger and skimmer,
my waxworms and fish bucket
huddle beside me. The wind
clips its swivel to my face.

The fish aren't biting.
I imagine them huddled
around my cold bait, moving slow.
It will take them all day.
I wait with the other ice fishermen,
bent over our holes as in prayer:

Let the fish leave their sleep
and rise up our poles;
let our fingers recover
their delicate grace;
let the patience of walleye and pike
remind us:
all cold things will melt,
all sleeping things wake,
keeping their proper seasons.

Trout

First, slit the belly open
and rinse it clean. Then,
fill it up with butter,
a slab of bacon,
and three fresh slivers of lemon.
Then, wrap it in a skin of foil,
slip it into the coals,
and wait.

When the stars begin to drift toward you
with their thin hooks,
trolling the watery sky,
when the lodgepole pines reel out and in,
resilient, jigging their needles,
when the ground itself,
spawning its dark shadows,
closes its earthy fist,
remove the trout from its burnt pouch
and eat. The night will settle in,
sweet, the thin air crisp as a fin.

Then, burn the bones
in the last available flame,
take one deep breath, and sleep.
Nothing, now, can haunt you.

V. The Moon and Our Own Devices

Building a Workbench

I suppose nails.
Some two-by-fours and a hammer.
Yes, I can imagine it.
I open the plans.
They are so simple a child.
I cannot read them.
They disintegrate in my clumsy
hands.

When I pick up the hammer
its head falls off,
leaving me with the stump.
The nails slip through my fingers,
awkward, insincere.
When I raise my voice
against the wood
it splits.

I'm sitting in the basement
with all the spells I cannot manage:
tape measure, plumb bob, T-square,
my hands full of splinters,
nailing here, joining there,
furious now,
building my workbench out of thin
air.

Making Do

The roofers are talking about
how they've brought the wrong materials.
The old one coughs a lump of asphalt
from his throat. The young one jingles
the nails of his teeth. They are
cutting corners, making do.

Sitting in my window overhead, I wonder:
some dark night with the wind swearing
it was not its fault, will my roof,
patched with syllables, break off,
loose me from its moorings,
leave me empty, unprotected,
in the most unnatural weather,
with all the wrong materials, making do?

The Real Thing

The sea was as blue as the sky
and your eyes were as blue as the sea.
Could I help it?
I was happy. We were in love.

And the jellyfish floating in on the tide?
And the gulls in their lovely remoteness?
Who could see through
the blue angle of their descent,
the accuracy of stinger and beak,
the sea in its cool movement,
swelling? Who could care?

Oh the sky was our limitless future,
and the rhythmic sea laving the beach
was our love going on, and forever.
Could I help it?

And the bright starfish trapped in the shallows?
And the sea urchins reft of their spines?
And the shells with their ears full of memories?
Who could care? We were young;
how could summer and language betray us,
leave us stranded in this blue season,
our tongues blunt as husks in our cheeks?

Hippopotamus

I am tired of wallowing
in this mud and my own hide.
If I were a poet
and not a hippopotamus
I could be anything I wanted.
A gazelle, for instance.
The word springs from my mouth,
grows graceful
legs and muscles:
gazelle, gazelle
it dances on its syllables.
Excited by flies,
I waddle over to my thick wife,
full of the secrets of poetry.

Bottom's Dream

Lost in symphonies of himself,
Bottom could not explain
the growth of oboes in his nose
or the size of his violin ears.
The bones of a vision stuck in his throat.
When he called to Quince
an ass trumpeted in the distance.
Puck drummed memory from his brain
but the dream still tickled:
he sneezed fairies
and fancied laying a queen.
With stranger songs to see by
he set out to weave Theseus a play.

One Hook

I knew it was too late
when these blue fish
moved coolly out of the painting.
Klee, what have we done? I said.
But he was fishing, madly fishing.
Make hooks, he said.

Some of the fish slipped smoothly
into the cunts of little girls.
Some hung ties around their necks
and worked for I.B.M.
Some raised hard fins
and swam on highways,
fishmouths honking like horns.

And everything they touched turned
to fish.
The stars wore slime,
the moon grew gills,
trees darted quickly away
in schools.
They ate the grass,
the weeds, the people,
like kelp,
and laid their eggs.
While sturgeons in white gowns
came out to round us up.

Klee! Klee! I said. What is happening?
What do we do?
But he was fishing,
madly fishing.
Make hooks, he said.

The Medicine Man's Confession

It is, of course, sheer fakery.
Far back in my throat,
that dark bag of tricks,
I keep the god's voice secret.
They think he speaks from the woods, but
this thin trill of my epiglottis is
his small, explainable throne.

They say I cure the sick, but
the evil spirits I suck out
are simply stones
I hide beneath my tongue
before the ritual. It is no miracle
when I spit them out,
solid as tiny bones.

And yet, there are occasions when
I hear the voices in the trees;
the animals seem to be more gentle toward me.
And sometimes when I dance
alone, out beyond the village,
the lisping sun insistent as a stone,
the god's voice soaring from my tongue,
it rains. Lord, it rains.

They tell me it's no small thing.

Restoring the Moon

1

Your daughter, not knowing any better,
reaches into the sky and plucks down the moon.
She turns that strange fruit over
and over in her pale, small hands.
Slowly, the night takes shape.
The moon in her hands turns plum purple,
slips into her cheek.
She sucks on its sweet juice.

2

Your son skips a thin stone
out over the lake, something
you're too old to do.
Once, twice, it rises: the full moon.

3

Two lovers are walking together
holding hands against the dark.
Although it has grown too dark to see them,
they remind you of someone you once knew.
They kiss. The sound of their kiss rises above them
like a soft mist, like a bubble,
like the moon.

4

The sky is blank, a dark water.
The thin moon drifts through it like a hook,
jigging hypnotically. You swim over to it.
You strike.

5

You land on the moon.
It is not what it seems. Just rocks and dust.
Still, they are counting on you.
You reach in your pockets. Luckily, you've brought
your plums, stones, kisses, and hooks
with you. You take them out. You get to work.

Driving On into the Dark

I downshifted. The Volkswagen fell
into potholes and out
as we clung to its back,
clutching for all we were worth.
The moon-cratered road
rose up toward the moon.
We thought we could catch
the sun at the top
before the dark earth fell through.

Halfway, shadows of cows
held the dark in their teeth,
chewing slowly so we couldn't pass.
We tried all the spells: Shoo Boss!
Vamoose! Rumplestiltskin! Amen!
the Volkswagen folding its horn,
its loud eyes removing the dark,   .
until the cows finally
broke up in flakes
of dusk, and fell off the road.
We moved through the moony landscape.

Soon, the wheels broke away,
sailing off in their own constellations;
the fenders, distended, burst;
the seat belts turned to dust.
We tried to start back
but the trees picked us up
and drove us on into the night.
At the top of the rise

the balsamroot tuned up the grass;
the lupine cleared its blue throat.
While light years away,
behind Mount Moran,
the sun made its final betrayal:
leaving the dark, the musical dark,
to the moon and our own devices.